First Look:
Science

The Drop Goes Plop

A First Look at the Water Cycle

by Sam Godwin   illustrated by Simone Abel

Thanks to our reading adviser:

Susan Kesselring, M.A., Literacy Educator
Rosemount-Apple Valley-Eagan (Minnesota) School District

PICTURE WINDOW BOOKS
Minneapolis, Minnesota

First American edition published in 2005 by
Picture Window Books, a Capstone imprint
151 Good Counsel Drive
P.O. Box 669
Mankato, MN 56002-0669
877-845-8392
www.capstonepub.com

First published in Great Britain in 1998 by Macdonald Young Books,
an imprint of Wayland Publishers Ltd.
Reprinted in 2001 and 2002 by Hodder Wayland,
Hodder Children's Books
A division of Hodder Headline Limited
338 Euston Road
London NW1 3BH

Library of Congress Cataloging-in-Publication Data
Godwin, Sam.
The drop goes plop : a first look at the water cycle / by Sam
Godwin ; illustrated by Simone Abel.
p. cm.—(First look : science)
ISBN 13: 978-1-4048-0657-3 (hardcover)
ISBN 10: 1-4048-0657-1 (hardcover)
1. Hydrologic cycle—Juvenile literature. I. Abel, Simone, ill.
II. Title. III. Series.
GB848.G64 2005
551.48—dc22   2004007318

Printed in the United States of America in North Mankato, Minnesota.
012011   006069R

For all the raindrops at Burgess Hill School – SG

Thanks for everything John and Pamela – SA

A cloud forms high up in the sky. It grows bigger

4

over hills and fields and little towns.

7

Raindrops fall from the cloud. The drop

I'm singing in the rain!

When the cloud gets heavy, the drops fall out as rain. If it is really cold, the drops freeze and fall as snow or hail.

8

goes plop. It runs down the baby gull's feathers.

9

Down, down, down falls the drop

until—splash—it lands in a flowing river.

The drop is carried along the river—past houses

and under

bridges.

Rivers start as tiny streams on mountains. They are filled with water from lakes and springs. Rain falls and adds more water to the rivers.

At last, the drop floats into a peaceful reservoir.

A reservoir is a lake with a dam at one end. Water is stored here until people need it.

Then a dam is opened.

Poor drop! It is sucked into a water treatment plant

Water has to be cleaned before humans can use it because dirty water can make people sick.

and pushed up a pipe into a water tower. Where is it going now?

The shampoo bubbles foam and splatter!

19

The drop swishes around and around the tub. It swirls down the drain.

20

Poor drop! It whooshes down a pipe into the sewers.

At the water treatment plant, the drop travels through tanks and filters. It is squeaky clean again.

22

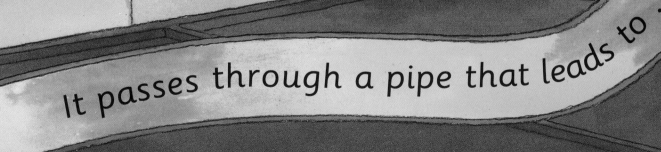

Water gets dirty after it has been used and has to be cleaned again.

It passes through a pipe that leads to . . .

THE SEA! The drop rises up into the air again.

24

Then the drop goes plop.

Its amazing journey starts all over again.

27

The Water Cycle

In the sky, water cools, and water droplets form clouds.

Water rises up from trees and plants.

Water is heated by the sun and rises up from the sea.

28

Useful Words

Dam
An enormous wall built to keep water in a reservoir.

Filter
A container of sand and gravel that is used to clean water. As water passes through the filter, dirt sticks to the sand and gravel.

Reservoir
A huge lake that has been especially made to store water.

River
A large stream of water. Rivers start as small streams on top of hills or mountains. As a river flows, it gets wider and deeper. It eventually flows into the sea.

Sewer
An underground system of drains and pipes that carries used water from our homes. The dirty water passes to a water treatment plant where it is cleaned before it is pumped into the sea.

Water Treatment Plant
A place where water from rivers and reservoirs is cleaned for people to use at home.

Fun Facts

- Earth has the same amount of water on it now as when it was formed.

- About 97 percent of the world's water is salty or undrinkable.

- A person can go an entire month without food, but only a week without water.

- When you brush your teeth, you use 2 gallons (7.6 liters) of water. You use between 25 and 50 gallons (95 and 190 liters) to take a shower.

To Learn More

At the Library

Berger, Melvin. *Water, Water Everywhere: A Book About the Water Cycle.* Nashville, Tenn.: Ideals Children's Books, 1995.

Frost, Helen. *The Water Cycle.* Mankato, Minn.: Pebble Books, 2000.

McKinney, Barbara Shaw. *A Drop Around the World.* Nevada City, Calif.: Dawn Publishing, 1998.

On the Web

FactHound offers a safe, fun way to find Web sites related to this book. All of the sites on FactHound have been researched by our staff.

1. Visit *www.facthound.com*
2. Type in this special code: 1404806571
3. Click the FETCH IT button.

Your trusty FactHound will fetch the best Web sites for you!

Index

Look for all the books in this series:

A Seed in Need
A First Look at the Plant Cycle

Paint a Sun in the Sky
A First Look at the Seasons

The Drop Goes Plop
A First Look at the Water Cycle

And Everyone Shouted, "Pull!"
A First Look at Forces of Motion

Take a Walk on a Rainbow
A First Look at Color

The Hen Can't Help It
A First Look at the Life Cycle of a Chicken

From Little Acorns …
A First Look at the Life Cycle of a Tree

The Case of the Missing Caterpillar
A First Look at the Life Cycle of a Butterfly

The Trouble with Tadpoles
A First Look at the Life Cycle of a Frog